GET RICH QUICK

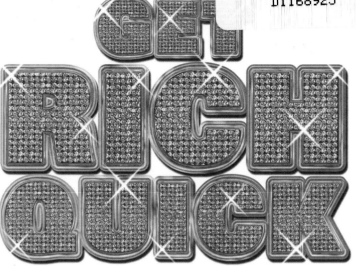

TOP THAT! Kids™

Published by Top That! Publishing plc
Tide Mill Way, Woodbridge, Suffolk, IP12 1AP, UK
www.topthatkids.com
Copyright © 2008 Top That! Publishing plc
Top That! Kids is a trademark of Top That! Publishing plc
0 2 4 6 8 9 7 5 3 1
Printed and bound in China.

What Is a Business?

So, you want to enter the world of commerce? Or at least, you think you do—but what's it all about?

A business is any operation you set up to try to make some extra money. You may get an allowance from your family, but that's not really a business, as you're pretty sure you're going to get the same amount of money every month, unless you're extra helpful or extra disobedient.

However, if you decide to use your allowance to make more money, then you've taken your first steps into business. You don't even have to have finances to set up a business (although you'll see on page 7 that it helps). Most businesses are built around a commodity and in your case, your basic commodity is YOU!

THE BIG PICTURE

What Is a Commodity?

It's something that can be used to your advantage or profit. The reason you are a commodity is that you have skills to offer to others, and are prepared to make the time to offer them.

Your mom may have superb oil painting skills, but if she's too busy working and looking after the family to pick up a paintbrush, it's not a commodity.

BEFORE YOU START!

TELL YOUR PARENTS WHAT YOU ARE DOING. NEVER LEAVE YOUR HOUSE OR NEIGHBORHOOD WITHOUT TELLING YOUR PARENTS WHERE YOU ARE GOING. IT'S BEST TO HAVE AN ADULT WITH YOU IF YOU ARE CONTACTING STRANGERS.

What Do You Enjoy?

The best idea is to turn a hobby into a business. That way, you already know something about your chosen subject, and you will be glad to spend your spare time doing it. It's unlikely your business will succeed if you offer computer services when really you'd rather be outside raking leaves or mowing lawns.

Can It Be a Business?

Your chosen hobby or business venture needs to be something that other people will pay for. Why would people give you money to listen to the radio all day? On the other hand, if you have a huge CD collection, they may pay for your services as a DJ at parties.

What Kind of Business?

All successful businesses have a purpose behind their main idea. To make any money, you need to persuade other people that you have something they need and want.

Take a look through the ideas on pages 15–31. They are all jobs that you can do which will help make other people's lives easier or better.
You can charge good money for these services, so long as your work is professional and good.
Do any of your business ideas match your hobbies, or skills that you already have?

COMPUTER WHIZ!
COMPUTER WHIZ!
COMPUTER WHIZ!
COMPUTER WHIZ!

People of the Business

Before you offer your services, decide who is to be involved in your business venture. Always have an adult as a mentor, someone you can turn to for advice and support. This could be a parent, teacher, youth group or church leader, or any adult you trust and know well, like an uncle or aunt.

BEFORE YOU START!
ALWAYS CHECK WITH YOUR PARENTS OR MENTOR BEFORE MAKING BUSINESS DECISIONS.

Some operations will work better if you have a partner. A partner will want to share any profits you make, but could help you make much more money overall. A double act may be more appealing as entertainers at a party. Extra people in a babysitting service means you won't have to turn away clients if you're already booked.

You may find that a friend is really good at running a business, and you're really good at arts and crafts. You could spend your time doing what you're best at, and your business partner could organize the tasks that bore you.

Don't forget, too, that there's safety in numbers. If you're working in someone else's home or yard, it's much safer to be there with a friend.

THE BIG PICTURE

The Business Plan

A good business starts with a good idea, but to make it work properly you need to plan ahead. Do you need a company name, or have you got a new service which needs a catchy name? How are you going to let people know about your business? Who will your business appeal to? What supplies will you need? What hours can you work? Do you need to check any legal requirements?

It's the Law

According to U.S. Law, a person of any age can do certain jobs, such as delivering newspapers. In most places, you should be able to offer simple services such as babysitting or cleaning. However, check that you're not breaking any laws before you start your business. You can look online for official local and federal guidelines. Check with your government to see if your business needs a license or permit, and that you're not breaking any rules. Find out, too, if there are any tax requirements once you start to charge for your services.

Business Budgets

The whole idea of running a business is to make a profit. That means you earn more money than you spend! You need to write down all the money you think you will use in your business.

Payables

This is money you spend on your business. If you plan to make things and sell them, you know that you will have to buy materials to work with. Write down all the items that cost money, and how often you have to buy them, to work out a monthly total.

Your payables will also include things like stationery (paper, printer ink, and so on), postage (if you have items which need delivering, or if you have to send people bills through the mail), and extras like travel (bus fares or gas if you ask your parents to drive you).

Receivables

This is more fun! Your receivables are the money your business earns.

Think carefully about what you will charge for your services or goods. Do some local research. People won't pay you twice as much to wash their car as it costs them at the gas station. On the other hand, it's no good charging fifty cents for homemade cookies, if the ingredients cost you more than that.

Record Keeping

When you have decided what your business will cost, and how much you will charge, write it all down for future reference. Every time you spend some money on your business, keep a record.

Keep careful notes of what prices you charge your customers. They won't be too happy if your price changes every time they ask you to work for them. Make it clear what the price includes. You may have to charge extra if you send their goods through the mail instead of delivering them by hand.

Your babysitting fee may go up if they are back later than they promised, or you may charge a lower hourly rate if they book you for a whole day on the weekend or during vacation time.

Bookkeeping

It's important that you keep a special notebook, or computer file, with all the details of your money. You need to know exactly how much you have spent, and how much you have earned. Your business is not a success if you've sold fifty friendship bracelets for a dollar each, but spent sixty dollars on thread, gift boxes, postage, and advertising!

Professional Conduct

All business people have to deal with the general public. You MUST be polite to them. Nobody will buy something from a rude person, even if he or she really likes it. If you lie to somebody, or go back on your word, he or she will stop asking you for your help or your products. Even worse, a disappointed customer might tell everyone he or she knows to stop using your business.

Negotiations

When you speak to people, don't expect them to agree with you all the time. They might not want to buy from you, or they may say you're too expensive. Be prepared to change your rules or prices a little—this is called negotiating. Offer a lower price if they buy more of your goods. Say you will charge a special rate for washing their car, if they promise to let you wash it once every month for the next six months.

Be Flexible

Accept that some people will just say no, whatever deal you offer. If they don't have children, they don't need babysitting services! You could politely ask them to recommend you to their friends, though. In the same way, if they don't need their lawn mowed right now, ask when would be a good time for you to check with them again.

Business Safety

It can't be said enough: stay safe whenever you're out and about running your business. Remember the basic rules (as shown in the gold seal on page 11).

These rules apply whether you're spending the day at someone's house (for example, if you're babysitting or cleaning), or whether you're visiting people to try to sell them things or tell them about your business.

Check your local laws carefully. In some places you have to be at least a certain age to sell from door to door, or you must have an adult accompanying you. This is for your own protection.

There are other ways you need to protect your business, too. You need to be sure that people will pay fairly for your goods and services, and not take advantage of you. If you're selling a product, always insist on cash on delivery. With a service, ask for payment at the end of each session. Don't babysit for a whole month before you ask for your money. It's too big a risk.

THE BIG PICTURE

Making the Time

Managing your time is one of the most important things you must learn as a business person. Your customers need to know that you won't be late, or forget to turn up altogether.

Before you promise to deliver an order, work out how long it will take you to make everything. If necessary, don't agree to a delivery date at first. Say that you will call your customer after you have taken ten minutes to plan the job, so you can be sure that you won't make a promise you can't keep.

If you arrange to be at a customer's house at a certain time, make sure you know how long it takes to get there. Try to arrive five minutes early so you don't keep them waiting.

WARNING!

TAKE SPECIAL CARE WHEN YOU HAVE CONTACT WITH STRANGERS.

ALWAYS TELL YOUR PARENTS WHERE YOU'RE GOING.

Keeping an Agenda

Use a notebook or your computer to keep track of all your appointments. Make a note of every single business arrangement you make, so that you can be sure you haven't promised to be in two places at the same time!

Marketing and Advertising

Before your business can make much money, people need to know that it exists. That's why you advertise what you do. Large businesses spend lots of money on things like TV and magazine ads, but you don't need to do that.

Speak Up

Tell all of your friends what you are doing, so that they can recommend you to people they know. Make good use of your parents' friends, as they're the ones most likely to need your product or service. If you do a job for a customer and he or she seems pleased with it, ask him or her to tell other people about what you do. This is called "networking"—setting up a whole group of people to spread the word on your behalf.

Play the Advantage

Use your age to get you noticed. If your business is doing well, tell your local newspaper and radio station about it. They might like to run a feature on your success story.

Special Promotions

One of the main, and most simple, reasons that people don't buy from a business is that they don't know it exists, or what it has to offer. You have to tell them what you do, and why you can be of use to them.

Samples and Coupons

Give out a few free samples of your product — this is a good way to attract business. You could also offer coupons for new potential customers such as "2 for 1" or "buy one, get one free" for the service you provide.

Fliers

Design a simple poster to deliver in your neighborhood. Write and draw it very neatly, and photocopy it, or design it on a computer and print it out. (Don't forget to include the money this costs in your record keeping.) Your poster, or flier, should contain your name (and company name), what your business does, and how to get in touch with you (an address, phone number, or e-mail address). Keep it simple so people don't get bored before they finish reading it.

Business Cards

Make your own small cards to give to people who know a little bit about your business. The cards only need your name and company, a telephone number, and maybe one line reminding people what you do, such as, "Your friendly, local babysitter" or "Computer repairs are our specialty." Leave a card after you've done a job, so satisfied customers can contact you again. Carry some in your wallet in case you meet new clients and want to give them your details.

Raring to Go

Now you are ready to begin your business, you need to decide what you want to do. Look through the following ideas to see what best suits your skills and interests. There will be some that instantly grab your attention, and others you'd hate to do.

Think carefully about what you want to do, and make sure it doesn't interfere with schoolwork and other responsibilities you may have.

Make a list of your strengths and weaknesses. Start a business that works with your strengths; it is no good being a graphic designer if you hate computers!

Creative Fun

If you prefer working alone and patience is one of your skills, then a business such as making greeting cards, cleaning or babysitting could be perfect for you.

Outdoor Type

If you don't mind getting up early and will go outside in any weather, then play on these strengths by delivering newspapers, mowing lawns or walking dogs.

Loud and Proud

If you love being the center of attention and are outgoing, then working in the entertainment business may be for you. Become a DJ, stand-up comedian, or play a musical instrument to a crowd!

BUSINESS IDEAS

Lemonade Stand

Got a sure-fire recipe for delicious homemade lemonade? Then sell it to thirsty visitors at yard sales, school fairs, and charity events.

- Make sure that you're not breaking any laws by selling without a license.
- Work out the cost per cup of lemonade by adding up your costs for ingredients, ice, cups, travel, and other equipment (for example, your table or stand, decorations, and posters).
- Figure out beforehand whether you'll make the lemonade on site, or prepare lots in bulk to take with you.

Lawn Care

Several jobs you could do: raking leaves, mowing lawns, or shoveling snow in the winter.

- Advertise your services on a leaflet delivered to every house in your neighborhood.
- Charge per job or per hour. Take bookings in advance, and find out whether you can use the customer's tools or need to bring your own.

Graphic Design

People will pay high prices for skilled designers, if the work is good. Offer to design invitation cards, letterheads, and posters.

Computer Consultant

Turn your computer skills into a business opportunity! You'd be surprised how many people (especially adults) own a computer but don't know how to use it.

- Advertise your skills to train other people how to use the internet, or a word processing package, or any other aspect of the PC. Charge per hour or set a fee for a course of six or twelve lessons. Decide whether you want to teach in someone's home, or would prefer your client to visit you.
- Arrange to visit family members once a month to "spring clean" their PCs, backup important files, update their software, and organize their hard drives to keep them running efficiently. Unless you're very skilled, don't undertake technical repairs.
- Offer typing and word processing services. This could be to help with a backlog of work or a one-time deadline a customer needs to meet, such as typing up a college paper. Or you could offer to type monthly letters—don't forget to charge for stationery, printer cartridges, and general wear and tear on your computer if you're working on your own machine.

Recycling

Spread the word that you will dispose of other people's unwanted items for a small fee.

- Take glass, paper, metal, and fabric items to a recycling center.
- Save the better items until you have enough to hold a garage or yard sale.
- Restore items, such as furniture, and sell them for a profit.

BUSINESS IDEAS

Selling Books

Start up a business selling your family's secondhand books. Expand by offering to buy unwanted books from other people and then sell them for a small profit.

- Attend garage sales and yard sales to pick up bargains.
- Do some research on the internet to find out what kind of books are valuable if you sell them to collectors. You might see them for a couple of dollars and be able to sell them at auctions or fairs for more money.

Bicycle/Skateboard Repair

Does your mom constantly tell you that skateboarding is a useless hobby? Prove her wrong by using your interests to set up a business.

- Get permission to use the garage or a workshop for your repairs. Ask before you use any tools or equipment, too. You may have to agree to pay for any tools that get broken or worn out.
- Only accept jobs that you can safely fix. If you send back a repaired item that then injures somebody, you may find yourself in legal and financial trouble. Look over the broken item before you quote a price and agree to do the work.

Babysitting

It's best to start with kids you know, until you have some experience handling small children in their own homes. Draw up a business plan outlining your ground rules:

- What age groups you will work with (no babies in diapers?)
- What you will charge for different time slots (lower hourly rate for whole days? higher rates for late hours?)
- What hours you can work (no later than 9 pm on schooldays?)
- What about special requirements (a sandwich and a drink if you babysit between the hours of 4 and 6 pm?)
- Make sure you have transportation to and from your babysitting destination. Make sure you can keep all of your appointments without losing out on homework time.

Home Sitting

Many people don't like leaving their houses empty while they are away on business or on vacation. You could charge a small fee to visit every day and empty the mailbox, turn on house lights, open the drapes, and keep the house looking as if it's occupied. If you're old enough to stay home alone, you could even arrange to spend some evenings watching TV in the empty house, so potential burglars see signs of life and leave the place alone. Always make sure you can use a phone to get help in an emergency, and make sure your parents agree to let you do this job.

Pet Professionals

If you love animals, combine your hobby with a great business opportunity. Some of these jobs will be especially good if you want to train as a veterinarian or other animal worker when you're older.

Pet Sitting

Charge a small fee for taking a caged animal into your own home while its owner goes on vacation, or arrange to get a house key and visit your client's house every day to feed and care for his or her pet. If you're given a key to someone else's home, look after it, and always be sure to lock the door when you leave!

Walking Dogs

Many people don't have time to walk their dogs every day, but will pay you to give their dogs exercise. You could even take a dog with you if you deliver newspapers—earning two wages at once! Meet the dog first to make sure it's friendly and not too big or energetic for you to keep under control. Always make sure you're prepared and equipped to clean up any mess along the way!

BUSINESS IDEAS

Selling Fish

If your hobby is keeping fish, and you're lucky enough to have a pregnant female, do some research on how to keep the babies safe after they're born. Usually, they need to be kept apart from the adults so they don't get eaten. When they're big enough, you can sell them to other fish owners, or maybe even to pet stores.

Cleaning Animals

This is the most boring part of owning a pet for many people, so they'll pay good money to get someone else to do it! Draw up a price list for all the jobs you're willing to do: cleaning cages (big and small), grooming animals (long and short-haired), bathing dogs, and so on. Keep all the equipment you'll need in a clean, hygienic carrying case with your company name on it, and make sure it's spotless at all times.

Trading Cards

There are so many sets of trading cards available now, you'll have lots of possible customers right away! Ask around for unwanted duplicates, and pay a small fee for spare cards if necessary. When you have a good selection, you can advertise to sell to other collectors. If you have some collections yourself which are nearly complete, look out for your final missing cards. A full collection may be worth a lot of money if you sell it at a hobby fair or convention.

$ BUSINESS IDEAS

That's Entertainment

Are you a skilled musician or actor? Then you have a talent which could make you money! Other useful skills are magician, clown, storyteller, or even moviemaker!

- Decide how you will turn your talent into a money-making opportunity. Will you perform at children's parties? If so, you will need to work out and practice a really professional routine.
- If music is your thing, you could offer to perform at special events—think weddings, parties, bar mitzvahs, and more. You might be able to earn some extra money by teaching others, too!
- Whatever your talent, you should do some local research before you set your prices. Check out the competition to make sure you're not charging twice as much as they are.
- Ask if you can put up posters in music stores, kids' stores, and libraries.

Tutoring

Some parents will pay you to tutor their children in their weaker subjects. This is an especially good way for you to make money if you're a math genius, or speak a second language fluently.

- It's a good idea to speak to others with tutoring experience to get a feel for what you will need to do.
- Be prepared to commit to a long-term schedule of meeting once a week for a whole semester. Make sure this won't interfere with your own schoolwork.
- Agree on a price before you start the course of lessons.
Prepare your lessons well in advance, and check if you'll be required to help your student with his or her homework, or make up your own topics each week.

BUSINESS IDEAS

Wash and Go

Setting up your own car wash service is easy, quick, and inexpensive. It's flexible, too—you can also wash boats, RVs, and lawn furniture.

- As you'll be on other people's property while you work, try to have a cell phone with you in case of emergency. Let your parents know exactly where you're going to work.
- Carry all the equipment you'll need. Obviously, you'll need to ask the client for a hose and water.
- Practice on your parents' cars so you know how long it takes to do a good job. This will help you to decide how much to charge.

Worm Farmer

Do people really want to buy worms? Well, fishermen and gardeners might! Worms are great for use in composting, fertilizer, and as fishing bait. If you love the wriggly creatures and don't mind getting your hands dirty now and then, worm farming is a good, profitable hobby!

Read more on the internet about "vermiculture" to find out how to set up and care for your farm, and to make sure you sell healthy, happy worms.

Arts and Crafts

If you have creative skills, sell your products to friends and family, or at craft fairs, or over the internet. Make sure your prices cover all your costs (materials, delivery, gift wrap) and give you a profit for all the time you spend on an item. Charge more for an item that takes a week to make than you'd charge for an item you make in an hour. Here are some business ideas:

Drawing and Painting

Sell local landscapes or offer to paint portraits as presents.

Jewelry

You can charge high prices for good quality, unique designs.

Greeting Cards and Bookmarks

Make handmade paper products decorated with pressed flowers or other special designs.

Friendship Bracelets

Make your favorite designs in different colors, then take orders to make them in your customer's choice of color.

$ BUSINESS IDEAS

Puppet Maker

Remember to agree on a delivery date that you can realistically meet, allowing plenty of time for paint and glue to dry before you package an item.

Shirt Painter

Prepare a leaflet showing selected designs for customers to choose from, and have samples to show them the quality of your work.

Website Design/Maintenance

This is a new area of business, and many adults don't know much about setting things up online.

- Charge a set price for creating an online newsletter or magazine, or for designing and uploading a web site.
- Charge a separate fee for maintaining a web site (for example, adding new pages, or running a message board).
- Make sure that your customer tells you clearly what he or she wants it to look like, and warn him or her that you will charge extra if they change it when you're done. It's best to get their approval at a preliminary stage of design before going full speed. Make it clear that they need to supply all the information to go online,

including words, photographs and other pictures, prices, dates, etc.
- Be sure that your computer has enough space to hold all the information. You'll also need a reliable scanner and modem connection to make sure you don't let your customer down. Charge extra if you offer additional services like digital photography.

Cleaning Houses

Obviously, this involves you working in other people's homes, so stay safe at all times. Carry a cell phone and make sure your parents know where you are and what time you'll be home.

- Arrange to visit the house before you agree to do the job. Find out all the details about which rooms you should clean and what's expected of you. Are you simply vacuuming and dusting, or do you have to wipe down surfaces, mop floors, and clean windows?
- Change your prices depending on the number of rooms to be cleaned, the tasks involved, and whether you have to supply cleaning items such as polish.
- If you don't feel happy with the people on your first visit, don't agree to do the job.
- Arrange how often you will be needed, and be prepared to commit to regular visits over a number of months. Make sure it won't interfere with your schoolwork, and that you will be paid enough to make it worthwhile.

BUSINESS IDEAS

Green Thumbs

If you love growing things in your garden, you might be able to sell the results to make some extra money. Fruit, vegetables, and fresh flowers are all good to sell, especially today when many people prefer organic foods.

- Be careful, though, if you advertise as organic. There are strict guidelines about what this means.
- Set up a stall at local fairs or farmer's markets, or at the end of your driveway, displaying your produce. Make sure the items are well displayed and look their best.
- Sell the items already weighed in bags, or wrapped in bunches, for a set price. This price should be a little lower than in the main stores, as your items might be irregular shaped vegetables, or fruits which taste great but are smaller than store versions.

Fashion

Cool! Making money out of something that you usually spend all your cash on! Be prepared to fight long and hard against lots of competition, though, as many people want to be part of the fashion industry.

Modeling

Don't give up on this idea if you're not supermodel tall or willowy thin. Some agencies specialize in different-size models. There are also special agencies for hand-models and even foot-models. However, do some research on the internet before you consider even looking for an agency. Lots of people have lost money paying for expensive portfolios and sign up fees, and never get asked to attend a paying job. Being a model is very hard work and doesn't necessarily pay a lot. Be sure to discuss all decisions thoroughly with your parents.

Beauty Aid

Here's another idea that would look great on your resumé if you want to train in the beauty industry. Set up a manicure, pedicure, or facial service, and practice on your friends and family until you can do it really well.

- Use your own nailcare products, including handcream, nail polish remover, cotton balls, and disposable nail files. Always ask your customer first if she wants to use her own creams in case she is allergic to yours.
- Carry all of your equipment in a pretty vanity case. Make sure it is spotlessly clean at all times. Keep a supply of disinfectant wipes, and small plastic bags to throw away your garbage. To create the right impression, wear a white, short-sleeved shirt as a kind of uniform. Your customers need to be sure that your service is hygienic and safe.
- Make sure your customer is comfortable, and be prepared to make conversation while you work. Make sure that you find a comfortable position to sit in while you work, too, so you don't get a sore back, arms, or legs.

Fashion Consultant

If you have a good eye for color, and like to follow fashion, you could offer a service giving advice to other people. You can go shopping with them and pick out what they should be wearing, to suit their shape, size, and age, or to be super trendy. They may also pay you to do the shopping without them. First you find out what they like and what occasion they need an outfit for, then you choose a selection of clothes to take to their home.

Cooking and Baking

If your talents lie in the kitchen, you can easily make products that people will be willing to buy. Sell your cookies and cakes at local markets, or advertise that you will bake for special occasions such as birthday parties.

- Make sure your kitchen is clean and hygienic so you don't risk making your customers ill. Also remember to wash your hands before beginning to cook.

- Work out the price of your goods before you sell them. Include the cost of ingredients, delivery, or travel. Remember to add on extra if your cakes are decorated for special occasions and therefore take longer to make.

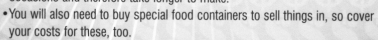

- You will also need to buy special food containers to sell things in, so cover your costs for these, too.

- Ask an adult to help you when using the stove or oven.

Gift Wrapping

Practice wrapping gifts until you can make them look professional and glamorous! Obviously, December will be one of your busiest months, but expect to have little work at other times. You will usually quote a price per present, based on size. Print out a price list of different gift wrap styles, and make sure you find out what design your customer wants. Your luxurious silver and gold wrapping might not be appreciated if your customer has a pile of children's toys to be wrapped!

Event Organizer

You might feel like you don't have a hobby or talent that could make you any money. If you're not creative, or a computer whiz, maybe you're a natural leader? Use your skills to get other people organized! Start by offering your services to people you know, including youth groups you belong to. Agree on an overall fee before you start, and arrange which costs come out of your fee, and which will be extra. For example, you might charge extra for photocopying posters and leaflets, but agree not to charge for any phone calls you make. You can organize other events when you get more confident, but it's often easiest if it's something you've experienced yourself. Organizing a business conference won't be so easy if you're still in school full time!

BUSINESS IDEAS

DJ

You'll need lots of equipment before you can offer your services as a DJ, as well as a huge album collection. You must be confident using CD players, as well as able to set up the whole sound system of speakers, amps, lights, and so on. Always make sure that the venue has enough electric sockets for all of your equipment! You should set a fee for a set time, but don't forget that you'll need to be there before and after to set up and put away. Practice introducing tunes and changing songs before you go into business. It's not as easy as you might think! When everyone is on the dance floor waiting for the next track, you're really under pressure! You should also make sure you've got a wide variety of music, from children's party songs to old-time classics, not just your own personal favorites. A good DJ can tell from his or her audience what's going to keep the dance floor busy, and what's going to empty it in no time!

BUSINESS IDEAS

Newspaper Delivery

This is a good way to get used to the world of work, since someone else organizes what you have to do, and you get a definite fixed income every week. Just contact your local paper for opportunities. It can be hard work, and you have to be reliable and show up every time, whatever the weather, and not be late. At least you don't need much equipment, though—generally just you and your bike!

- Make sure that if you are cycling in the dark you wear bright, or light clothes and that your cycle has lights on it.
- Always take care when cycling on the road and watch out for traffic and pedestrians.
- Keep newspapers and magazines in a waterproof bag so they don't get wet if it rains or snows.

Laundry Services

Offer to wash your customer's laundry for a small fee.
- Remember to wash colors and whites separately.
- You could go to a laundrette or use your washing machine at home. Make sure you ask whoever owns the machine first for permission.
- Charge slightly more to cover laundrette fees, soap, and for general wear and tear if you're using a machine at home.
- For a bit more money, offer your ironing services as well.

DECISION TIME

Ready to Succeed

Hopefully you're now full of ideas for your first steps into the business world. Even if your hobby isn't listed here, there should be something similar that will give you helpful advice on how to begin, set your prices, what to do about equipment, and how to stay safe when you're working outside your own home.

Further Research

Use the internet at home, school, or in the library to do research into your business idea. Make sure there isn't somebody just around the corner doing exactly what you want to do, compare your prices to other local businesses, and research places where you can advertise your product.

And Finally

Remember, the main points to being successful are:

- make people aware that you exist;
- be professional at all times;
- do a good job so that people will tell their friends and use you again and again!

If your business doesn't succeed the first time around, don't despair. Think about how you could improve upon what you have already done, or try again with something different.

Good luck!